# Halloween

## Dorothy Goeller

**Bailey Books**
an imprint of
**Enslow Publishers, Inc.**
40 Industrial Road
Box 398
Berkeley Heights, NJ 07922
USA
http://www.enslow.com

Bailey Books, an imprint of Enslow Publishers, Inc.

**Library of Congress Cataloging-in-Publication Data**

Goeller, Dorothy.
    Halloween / Dorothy Goeller.
        p. cm. — (All about holidays)
    Includes index.
    Summary: "Simple text and photographs present a story with a Halloween theme"
    —Provided by publisher.
    ISBN 978-0-7660-3807-3
    1. Halloween—Juvenile literature. I. Title.
    GT4965.G64 2011
    394.2646—dc22

                                          2010012568

Paperback ISBN: 978-1-59845-176-4

Printed in the United States of America

062010 Lake Book Manufacturing, Inc., Melrose Park, IL

10 9 8 7 6 5 4 3 2 1

# Note to Parents and Teachers

Help pre-readers get a jumpstart on reading. These lively stories introduce simple concepts
with repetition of words and short simple sentences. Photos and illustrations fill the pages
with color and effectively enhance the text. Free Educator Guides are available for this
series at www.enslow.com. Search for the *All About Holidays* series name.

# Contents

# Words to Know

boo

**not**    **who**

# Who says boo?

# Not I!

# Not I!

# Not I!

# Not I!

# Not I!

# Not I!

# Not I!

# Not I!

# But I do!

# Read More

———. *Five Little Pumpkins*. New York: HarperFestival, 1998.

dePaola, Tomie. *My First Halloween*. New York: Grosset & Dunlap, 2008.

# Web Sites

Kaboose. *Halloween Recipes and Halloween Activities*. <http://holidays.kaboose.com/halloween/>

Family Fun. *Halloween Games for the Family*. <familyfun.go.com/halloween/halloween-games>

# Index

Guided Reading Level: **B**
Guided Reading Leveling System is based on the guidelines recommended by Fountas and Pinnell.

Word Count: 22